KITCHEN MATH

Math and My World

Kieran Walsh

Rourke
Publishing LLC
Vero Beach, Florida 32964

© 2004 Rourke Publishing LLC

www.rourkepublishing.com

PHOTO CREDITS:
Cover photo by GettyImages.com. All other photos from AbleStock.com, except for p. 34 by the author and illustration of woman cooking © Getty Images™

Editor: Frank Sloan

Cover and interior design by Nicola Stratford
Page layout by Heather Scarborough

Library of Congress Cataloging-in-Publication Data

Walsh, Kieran.
  Kitchen math / by Kieran Walsh.
     p. cm. -- (Math and my world)
Includes bibliographical references and index.
Contents: Recipes and units of measure -- Dry measure and liquid measure
-- The metric system -- Refrigeration and freezing -- Cooking --
"Nutrition facts" food labels -- Calories.
  ISBN 1-58952-382-2 (hardcover)
 1. Mathematics--Study and teaching (Elementary)--Juvenile literature.
2. Cooking--Juvenile literature. [1. Mathematics. 2. Cookery. 3.
Weights and measures.] I. Title. II. Series: Walsh, Kieran. Math and
my world.
  QA135.6.W32 2003
  641.5'01'51--dc22
                                              2003011562

Printed in the USA

w/w

TABLE OF CONTENTS

Introduction 4

Recipes and Units of Measure 6

Dry Measure and Liquid Measure 14

The Metric System 20

Refrigeration and Freezing 24

Cooking 28

"Nutrition Facts" Food Labels 32

Calories 36

Nutrients 40

Conclusion 44

Glossary 46

Further Reading .47

Websites to Visit 47

Index 48

INTRODUCTION

People use math to work with food in all sorts of ways. When your parents buy food, for instance, they use math to figure out exactly how much the food they need to purchase will cost.

Have you ever helped your parents put away the groceries? Maybe you didn't know it, but by putting the food into the refrigerator, you were using math to keep the food fresh!

As you will see, the mathematics that applies to food ranges from simple to complex. Can you imagine some simple math that relates to food?

When your parents buy food, they use math to find out how much the food will cost. If these ears of corn, for instance, are 50 cents each, how much will five ears cost?

How about this—if you eat one slice of pizza, and then have another slice, how many slices of pizza have you eaten?

$$1 + 1 = 2$$

Two slices of pizza!

And, if there were eight slices of pizza to begin with, how many slices are left?

$$8 - 2 = 6$$

Six slices of pizza!

On the other hand, the math becomes very complex once you've eaten food. When food enters your body it travels to the stomach to be **digested**, or converted to energy. Math can give you an idea of how much energy you can expect to get out of a particular food!

To start with, though, you will need to know how math applies to the creation of food.

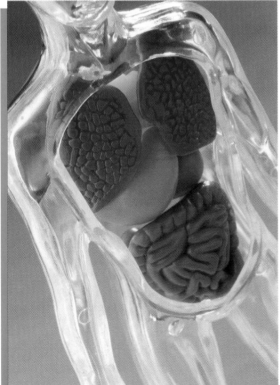

The stomach (in blue) is where food is digested, or broken down for use as fuel.

RECIPES AND UNITS OF MEASURE

Have you ever made a peanut butter and jelly sandwich? How did you do it?

Now think about this—how would you explain to someone else how to make a peanut butter and jelly sandwich?

You would probably say something like:

1) Get two slices of bread, peanut butter, and jelly

2) Spread some peanut butter on one slice of bread, and some jelly on the other slice of bread.

3) Put the two pieces of bread together, with the spreads on the inside, to make a sandwich. Guess what?

You may never have thought of them that way, but recipes are very much like mathematical formulas.

That's a **recipe**, a group of instructions telling someone how to make something. The bread, peanut butter, and jelly are all **ingredients** in the recipe.

The instructions for making a peanut butter and jelly sandwich are, obviously, a very simple recipe. Recipes can be simple or complex, but they always follow the same pattern. They specify a set of ingredients and tell you what to do with them to create the finished product.

What makes the peanut butter and jelly sandwich a simple recipe? Take a look at step 2. It says "spread *some* peanut butter on one slice of bread, and *some* jelly on the other slice of bread." That is partly why it is such a simple recipe. The amounts of peanut butter and jelly are not exact. It's basically up to you to decide how much you want to put on your sandwich. Another reason it's a simple recipe is because there are only three ingredients.

What about foods like tacos, or lasagna, or soup? These foods are made with more complicated recipes. They are complicated because they use many different ingredients and require very specific amounts of each. Determining an exact amount of something is called **measuring**.

Let's take a look at the ingredients in a complex recipe. Here are the ingredients in a recipe for chocolate brownies:

1/2 cup butter
1 cup white sugar
2 eggs
1 teaspoon vanilla extract
1/3 cup unsweetened cocoa powder
1/2 cup all-purpose flour
1/4 teaspoon salt
1/4 teaspoon baking powder

You can probably see the difference between this recipe and the recipe for the peanut butter sandwich. This recipe doesn't just say "some eggs," it calls for two eggs. You're dealing with exact amounts now.

A complex recipe involves lots of different ingredients and specifies exact measurements for each. What's the most complicated recipe you've ever made?

Likewise, you have probably noticed that this recipe uses terms like cup or tablespoon. These are **units of measure**. More specifically, cups and tablespoons are units of cooking measure.

The following are the units of cooking measure:

1 tablespoon (tbsp.) = 3 teaspoons (tsp.)
0.5 fluid ounce (fl. oz.)

1 cup = 8 fl. oz.
1 pint (pt.) = 2 cups
1 quart (qt.) = 2 pints
1 gallon (gal.) = 4 quarts
1 bushel (bu.) = 8 gallons

These units of cooking measure are useful because they make altering recipes very simple. For example, this brownie recipe makes about 16 brownies. What if you wanted to make twice that amount? All you would have to do is multiply the amounts of the ingredients by two.

Multiplication is a way of adding large groups of numbers. For instance, as you know, this recipe makes 16 brownies. What would twice that amount be? You can find out in a couple of different ways. You can add 16 and 16:

$$16 + 16 = 32$$

Or, you can use multiplication to get the same result:

$$2 \times 16 = 32$$

The example above is called a multiplication **equation**. In a multiplication equation, each number has a particular name. In this case, the number 2 is called the **multiplicand**. The number of brownies, 16, is the **multiplier**. Finally, the answer to your question, 32, is the **product**. So now you know that by doubling the ingredients in this recipe, you can make 32 brownies.

Now you'll work on the recipe itself. First of all, to make things easier, let's convert the ingredients that were expressed in fractions into decimal numbers. This is easy to do, since a fraction is really just another way of expressing a **division** problem. Take, for instance, the first item, 1/2 cup butter. This can also be expressed as a division equation:

$$1 \div 2 = .5$$

The numbers in a division equation also have names: 1 is the **dividend**, 2 is the **divisor**, and the answer, .5, is called the **quotient**.

Let's do this to all the fractions in your recipe:

1/2 cup butter = .5 cup butter

1 cup white sugar = 1 cup white sugar

2 eggs = 2 eggs

1 teaspoon vanilla extract =
1 teaspoon vanilla extract

1/3 cup unsweetened cocoa powder =
.33 cup unsweetened cocoa powder

1/2 cup all-purpose flour =
.5 cup all-purpose flour

1/4 teaspoon salt = .25 teaspoon salt

1/4 teaspoon baking powder =
.25 teaspoon baking powder

Now that you have converted your list of ingredients, you just have to multiply them by two:

.5 cup butter x 2 = 1 cup butter

1 cup white sugar x 2 = 2 cups white sugar

2 eggs x 2 = 4 eggs

1 teaspoon vanilla extract x 2 =
      2 teaspoons vanilla extract

.33 cup unsweetened cocoa powder x 2 =
      .66 cup unsweetened cocoa powder

.5 cup all-purpose flour x 2 = 1 cup all-purpose flour

.25 teaspoon salt x 2 = .5 teaspoon salt

.25 teaspoon baking powder x 2 =
      .5 teaspoon baking powder

Now you have a recipe for making 32 brownies!

<u>Small Amounts</u>

Some of the resulting numbers in that converted brownie recipe might seem a little strange to you. For instance, how would you measure .66 cup unsweetened cocoa powder? It's not so difficult, actually. Just remember that half a cup would be .5, so .66 is a little more than that, or 2/3 of a cup. Sometimes, though, a recipe will call for a *very* small amount of an ingredient. You might see terms like a *dash* of pepper, or a *pinch* of salt. These terms indicate quantities that are just too small for measure. Rather than specifying a ridiculously small amount, like, say, .000125 of a tablespoon, the amount to be added is left up to the cook—that's you!

DRY MEASURE AND LIQUID MEASURE

When following a recipe, you use cooking measures—tablespoons, cups, quarts, and gallons.

The standards for cooking measure apply to both dry quantities like flour and liquid quantities like milk. For instance, if you were making something that called for 1 cup of flour and 1 cup of milk, you could use the same cup to measure both ingredients.

A bowl of cereal is a very simple recipe that uses both dry quantities (cereal) and liquid quantities (milk).

However, if you look at these items in a supermarket, you'll see that they are measured in different ways. A container of milk isn't measured in cups—it is measured in gallons. Likewise, a bag of flour isn't measured in cups—it is measured in pounds.

Part of the reason for this difference is that cups are a relatively small amount. If all the items in a supermarket were measured in cups, there would have to be some very large numbers on the food labels!

Also, the items in a supermarket are usually divided into dry quantities and liquid quantities. Dry quantities include things like rice, flour, or cereal, while liquid quantities include milk, soda, and orange juice.

Liquid quantities are measured according to liquid volume or capacity. The units of measure for liquid quantities are the same as cooking measurements:

1 tablespoon (tbsp.) = 3 teaspoons (tsp.)
  0.5 fluid ounce (fl. oz.)
1 cup = 8 fl. oz.
1 pint (pt.) = 2 cups
1 quart (qt.) = 2 pints
1 gallon (gal.) = 4 quarts
1 bushel (bu.) = 8 gallons

Using this chart, can you determine how many cups are in a half-gallon container of milk?

To begin with, isolate the section of the chart dealing with cups up to gallons:

1 cup = 8 fl. oz.
1 pint (pt.) = 2 cups
1 quart (qt.) = 2 pints
1 gallon (gal.) = 4 quarts

Working backward and using multiplication, you can determine how many cups are in 1 gallon:

1 gallon = 4 quarts

4 x (1 quart = 2 pints) gives 4 quarts = 8 pints

8 x (1 pint = 2 cups) gives 8 pints = 16 cups

So, if there are 16 cups to a gallon, you can find out the number of cups in a half-gallon by dividing this result by 2:

$$16 \div 2 = 8$$

A half-gallon container of milk contains about 8 cups!

Dry quantities, on the other hand, are usually measured by **weight**. Dry quantities include items like butter, rice, and cereal.

For instance, here is the weight label from a standard jar of peanut butter:

NET WT. 18 OZ.

(1 LB. 2 OZ.)

What does all that mean?

First of all, NET WT can be read as *net weight*.

OZ, meanwhile, is an abbreviation for *ounces*. So, reading the first line aloud, you would say that the jar of peanut butter's net weight is eighteen ounces.

Concentrate on the second line. LB is the abbreviation for *pound*. This line, therefore, can be read as one pound, two ounces.

Math will make this clearer. If the jar of peanut butter contains 18 ounces, and there are 16 ounces in a pound, then how many pounds of peanut butter are in the jar?

There are 18 ounces, so you know that the jar contains at least 1 pound of peanut butter. So what's left?

$$18 - 16 = 2$$

2 ounces!

Altogether, the jar of peanut butter contains 18 ounces, or one pound, 2 ounces of peanut butter!

How about a box of cereal that contains 21 ounces of cereal? How would you express that in pounds?

$$21 - 16 = 5$$

The box of cereal contains 1 pound, 5 ounces of cereal!

Meats and fish are always measured in pounds. If each of these fish weigh roughly 1/2 pound, and they are priced at $7 a pound, how much would it cost to buy three fish?

Meats and Fish

Weight is also the system of measurement for foods such as ground beef, chicken, cold meats, and fish. If you have ever gone to a butcher's shop, or seen how a deli counter works, you've heard people asking for meats in terms of "a half pound of turkey" or "a quarter pound of roast beef." What these people are actually doing is expressing fractions:

A half pound of turkey = 1/2 LB. of turkey

A quarter pound of roast beef = 1/4 LB. of roast beef

THE METRIC SYSTEM

We actually have two systems of weights and measure in the United States. Quarts, pints, gallons, ounces, and pounds are all units of the U.S. Customary System, also known as the English System.

The other system of measurement, and the only one sanctioned by the United States Government, is the **metric system**, which is also known as the International System of Units.

Most of the world uses the metric system. If you were to do your shopping at a grocery store in Europe, for example, all of the dry quantities would be measured in grams, while the liquid quantities would be measured in liters.

Meanwhile, the items in an American supermarket are actually measured in both systems. For instance, here are the specifications for a tub of butter:

NET WT 1LB (453 g)

You know that this means the net weight of the tub of butter is 1 pound. But what about that other number, 453 g?

The "g" is simply an abbreviation for "grams," a metric unit of dry measure. The tub of butter contains 1 pound of butter, which can also be measured as 453 grams of butter.

Here are the units for converting between the U.S. Customary System of Measure and the metric system:

Dry Measure	Liquid Measure
1 ounce = 28.3495 grams	1 cup = 0.236 liters
1 pound = 453.59 grams	1 pint = 0.473 liters
	1 quart = 0.946 liters
	1 gallon = 3.78 liters

(reproduced from 2000 New York Times Almanac)

If you have two pounds of flour, how many grams is that equal to?

Using this table, you can do some math to convert the quantities used in the United States to something people in the rest of the world can understand.

If a box of rice contains 7 ounces of rice, how many grams is that?

You can find out by using multiplication. You know that 1 ounce is equal to 28.3 grams, so:

$$7 \text{ (ounces)} \times 28.3 = 198.1 \text{ grams}$$

7 ounces of rice is equal to 198 grams of rice!

What about a half-gallon of milk? How much would that be expressed in liters? To figure this out, you can use division. You know that 1 gallon is equal to 3.78 liters. So if you divide 3.78 by 2:

$$3.78 \div 2 = 1.89$$

Therefore, a half-gallon of milk is about 1.89 liters of milk. As you can see, the metric system is really pretty simple, once you get used to it.

The Creation of the Metric System

French scientists developed the metric system during the 1790s. The basic unit of measurement in the metric system is the meter, which is about one ten-millionth the distance from the North Pole to the equator. A metal bar used to represent the length of the standard meter was even created. This bar was replaced in the 1980s, though, when scientists changed the standard of measurement for the meter to a portion of the distance traveled by light in a vacuum.

If one meter is roughly equal to one ten-millionth the distance between the North Pole and the equator, and one meter is also equal to about 39 inches, can you figure out how many inches there are from the North Pole to the equator?

REFRIGERATION AND FREEZING

Unfortunately, foods do not last forever. You know this if you have ever seen your parents throw away food that has gone bad.

You cannot stop food from spoiling, but you can delay it from happening. There are a couple of different ways to do this, and they are both at work in your kitchen.

What is the biggest appliance in your kitchen? Most likely, the biggest appliance in your kitchen, bigger than the toaster or the dishwasher or even the stove, is the refrigerator.

And, even though we call it a refrigerator, it is important to remember that it is really only half refrigerator. The other half is the freezer. The freezer portion is usually smaller than the refrigerator, though. This is why some families actually have a separate freezer where they can store larger quantities of foods.

The refrigerator and freezer are the most useful tools we have for keeping foods fresh. Foods spoil because of **bacteria** growth. You can slow down this process by keeping foods in the refrigerator. In the refrigerator, the low temperature slows down the growth of bacteria.

The temperature inside of a refrigerator or freezer is much lower than that of room temperature— the temperature where human beings feel comfortable. Room temperature is typically about 72 degrees Fahrenheit.

The temperature in your family's kitchen is probably close to room temperature (72°), but the temperature inside appliances like the stove and the refrigerator will be different.

What about the temperature inside the refrigerator? The normal, or recommended, temperature for inside the refrigerator is about 35 degrees Fahrenheit.

How much lower is the temperature inside the refrigerator compared to room temperature? You can find out by using subtraction:

$$72 - 35 = 37$$

The temperature inside the refrigerator is about 37 degrees Fahrenheit lower than room temperature.

Now how about the temperature inside the freezer? The normal, recommended temperature inside a freezer is about 4 degrees Fahrenheit.

How much lower is the temperature inside the freezer compared to room temperature? Again, you can find out by using subtraction:

$$72 - 4 = 68$$

The temperature inside the freezer is about 68 degrees lower than room temperature.
That's pretty cold!

And how do the temperatures of the refrigerator and freezer compare to each other? You can find out by subtracting the lower number (freezer temperature) from the higher number (refrigerator temperature):

$$35 - 4 = 31$$

So, you can say a couple of things about this. You can say that the temperature inside the freezer is 31 degrees Fahrenheit colder than that of the refrigerator. You can also say that the temperature inside the refrigerator is 31 degrees Fahrenheit warmer than that of the freezer. It all depends on how you look at it!

Expiration Dates

All food comes with an **expiration date** listed somewhere on the package. This date gives you an idea of when a food will start to spoil. It is a good idea to pay attention to the expiration date, especially when eating foods that spoil quickly, such as dairy products like milk or butter.

If it is the 16th of the month, and the tub of butter in your refrigerator has an expiration date of the 18th, how many more days is the butter good for?

$$18 - 16 = 2$$

The butter is good for two more days!

COOKING

Certain kinds of bacteria can make you very sick. So, obviously, bacteria is not something that you want in your food. This is why people refrigerate and freeze foods. It is also why people cook foods.

This is not true for every kind of food. For instance, people can eat vegetables raw or cooked. You can eat fruits, like apples, raw—or you can eat them cooked, as they would be inside an apple pie.

There are some cases, though, where cooking food is necessary. This is the case with meats, poultry (chicken), and eggs.

Refrigeration is a way of preventing the growth of bacteria by lowering the temperature. Cooking, meanwhile, is a way of killing bacteria that has already grown by raising the temperature.

All cooking is basically a question of heat transfer. Heat transfer is a scientific concept. There are three methods of heat transfer, including:
1) Conduction—the transfer of heat through solids
2) Convection—the transfer of heat through fluids
3) Radiation—the transfer of heat through space

Vegetables and fruits can be eaten raw or cooked. ▶
Which do you prefer?

Most methods of cooking fall into one of the first two categories. For instance, what if you wanted to cook some hot dogs? Frying the hot dogs in a pan on the stove would be cooking by conduction. On the other hand, if you filled the pan with water and boiled the hot dogs, that would be cooking by convection.

The kitchen stove is where people do most of their cooking. The burners on the stovetop are not marked with temperatures, though. Burners usually just have knobs indicating "LOW," "MED" (medium), and "HI" (high) settings. If you were to put a cooking thermometer on top of a grilling pan, though, you could tell what the temperature was, and it would be much higher than that of room temperature.

Cooking in the oven is much more specific. The knobs for the stove are very precise.

Usually, they list temperatures in increments of 50, like 300, 350, 400, 450, and so on.

What if a recipe for a cake told you to put the cake batter into the oven for 55 minutes at a temperature of 350 degrees? How much higher would the temperature in the oven be compared to room temperature?

$$350 - 72 = 278$$

So, the temperature in an oven heated to 350 degrees is about 278 degrees higher than room temperature. No living thing, not even bacteria, could survive at a temperature that high.

The "burners" on a stove do not specify temperatures, but you can make some guesses. For instance, if the boiling point for water is 212°, how hot would you say the burner under this kettle is?

If the temperature in this oven is 450°, how much hotter is that compared to room temperature?

The Microwave

Since their introduction more than 20 years ago, microwaves have become steadily more popular. Nowadays, a microwave is a standard item in most kitchens — as common as the sink or a blender or a toaster oven.

It might seem like microwaves are an example of the third type of heat transfer, radiation—the transfer of heat through space, but they are really just another kind of stove. Instead of using heat, though, microwaves cook foods using radio waves. The radio waves excite the atoms in food, causing the food to get hot.

"NUTRITION FACTS" FOOD LABELS

How many meals do you eat in a day?

You probably said three—breakfast, lunch, and dinner.

This is the schedule most people stick to. They eat breakfast in the morning, lunch in the afternoon, and dinner in the evening.

But, have you ever skipped a meal? If so, what happened?

Right! You got hungry. But why?

The answer is simple. Food is our body's fuel. The word fuel should make you think of a car. Cars cannot run without fuel. Likewise, our bodies cannot work without food. Hunger is really our body's way of saying, "feed me!" We stick to a regular eating schedule for the same reason people don't wait until their car is out of gas to fill it back up.

Like gasoline for a car, food is our body's "fuel." Can you think of different ways that you use that fuel?

We eat because food enables our bodies to do all sorts of things, like grow, breathe, think, and repair tissue. In tissue. In short, food provides us with the nourishment that we need to live.

Do you have a favorite food? What is it? Maybe you said broccoli. Maybe you said chocolate!

In a perfect world, broccoli and chocolate would have the same nutritional value. In other words, the nourishment that you could get from a chocolate bar would be the same as that of a stalk of broccoli.

Unfortunately, this isn't the case. Some foods are just plain better for us than others.

The difference between broccoli and chocolate is pretty obvious. For some foods, though, the difference isn't so clear. This is where nutritional labels come in handy.

Ice cream is delicious, but it isn't the most nutritious food available. Some foods are better for us than others.

Nutrition Facts food labels give us a summary of what is good and bad about a particular food. These labels are especially useful when you consider how much of what we eat is made of several different foods.

For instance, what goes into a pie? It is made of several different things, including sugar, flour, fruit… and many other ingredients. It is fairly simple to say how nutritious one of those ingredients is, but with the Nutrition Facts label you can see how nutritious all of those ingredients are in combination.

A food label looks complicated, but it becomes a little more manageable if you break it down into sections. A typical food label is basically made of three sections:

1) Serving Size
2) **Calories**
3) **Nutrients**

Let's look at a real food label. In this case, it is a food label from a can of soup.

Nutrition Facts		
Serving Size 1 cup (240mL)		
Servings Per Container about 2		
Amount Per Serving		
Calories 150	Calories from Fat 25	
		% Daily Value*
Total Fat 2.5g		4%
Saturated Fat 1.5g		8%
Cholesterol 10mg		3%
Sodium 960mg		40%
Total Carbohydrate 24g		8%
Dietary Fiber 2g		8%
Sugars 5g		
Protein 9g		
Vitamin A 70%	•	Vitamin C 0%
Calcium 2%	•	Iron 6%

* Percent Daily Values are based on a 2,000 calorie diet. Your daily values may be higher or lower depending on your calorie needs:

	Calories:	2,000	2,500
Total Fat	Less than	65g	80g
Sat Fat	Less than	20g	25g
Cholesterol	Less than	300mg	300mg
Sodium	Less than	2,400mg	2,400mg
Total Carbohydrate		300g	375g
Dietary Fiber		25g	30g

"Nutrition Facts" food labels contain all the information you need to make decisions for healthy eating.

The first section, the Serving Size, should seem familiar to you. That is because it is based on the units of cooking measure. In this case, the can of soup, the Serving Size reads:

Serving Size 1 cup (240mL)

Servings Per Container about 2

So there are roughly two cups of soup in the can. It is important to understand this, because all the numbers that follow are all based on the serving size of *one* cup. In other words, if you ate the entire can of soup, you would be getting *twice* the amount of calories, sodium, and cholesterol listed.

Let's focus on what the nutrition label says for Sugar:

Sugars 5g

So you know that one serving (1 cup of soup) contains about 5 grams of sugar. But how much sugar would you be getting if you ate the entire can?

$$5 \text{ grams} \times 2 = 10 \text{ grams}$$

If you ate the whole can of soup, you would get about 10 grams of sugar!

CALORIES

You have probably heard of people "counting calories" in order to lose weight. But what are calories anyway?

Strictly speaking, a calorie is a measurement of heat energy. Remember the metric system? A calorie is the amount of heat needed to raise the temperature of 1 gram of pure water 1 degree centigrade. You already know that a gram is a metric unit of measurement. Centigrade, meanwhile, is simply another way of measuring temperature.

The body stores excess calories as fat, which is how people gain weight.

Foods that are high in calories contain a lot of potential energy, but if you don't use that energy, the body stores it as fat and you gain weight.

The concern over body weight, and the important role calories play in it, is why calories are listed at the top of a nutrition label.

The Calories section of a label, in this case, the label from the can of soup, looks like this:

Calories 150   Calories from Fat 25

"Calories from Fat" is another number people pay attention to if they are trying to lose weight.

In this case, what percentage of the can of soup is fat? You can find out by using division.

First of all, divide 25 by 150:

$$25 \div 150 = .16$$

Then, multiply the result by 100 to express it as a percentage:

$$.16 \times 100 = 16$$

So, 16% of the calories are from fat.

To put it simply, the less fat, the better: 16% isn't too bad. If you were to look at the "Calories from Fat" on a stick of butter though, it would probably say that 100% of the calories were from fat. That's a lot of fat!

The 2,000 Calorie Diet

    The amount of calories a person should eat in a day depends on a lot of different factors. These include the person's overall health, including his or her present weight, the type of work he or she does, and the amount of exercise he or she gets. People who work in manual labor or exercise on a regular basis need more calories than people who don't. But, for the most part, 2,000 calories is about what the average person should consume in a single day. That is what is meant by a "2,000 calorie diet."

    Using that measure, if you ate 1 cup of soup at 150 calories, how many calories would you have left for the day?

        $2000 - 150 = 1850$

        1,850 calories!

Exercise is a great way to burn calories. The important thing is to find a type of exercise that you enjoy.

NUTRIENTS

The next section of the nutrition label is about nutrients. Nutrients are the components of food, or what food is made of. In a sense, food is really just a container for nutrients. In the same way that you buy a can of soup for the food inside, you eat a food to get the nutrients inside of it.

They might look like apples, but they are really just "containers" of nutrients.

Look again at the label from the soup can. This time, though, focus on the section starting after where the Calories are listed. This is the Nutrients section, and you'll notice right away that there is a lot of math here. To the right of each of the different nutrients are percentages.

You've also probably noticed that this particular section of the food label seems to be split in half. On the top are nutrients like Total Fat, Cholesterol, and Sodium, while on the bottom are nutrients like Vitamin A, Vitamin C, and Iron.

Basically, the thing to understand here is that the top section lists nutrients that you probably get enough of already, while the bottom nutrients are ones you should make sure you get enough of.

And, as with calories, the numbers listed for these nutrients are based on the 2,000 calorie diet. In the previous section we only talked about this reference in terms of calories, but now look at what it says regarding nutrients:

Total Fat – Less than 65g
Sat (Saturated) Fat – Less than 20g
Cholesterol – Less than 300 mg
Sodium – Less than 2,400 mg
Total Carbohydrate – 300g
Dietary Fiber – 25g

Your can of soup contains 2.5 grams of Total Fat. What percentage of your daily allowance of fat would this be, based on the 2,000 calorie diet?

First of all, you know that the 2,000 calorie diet recommends less than 65 grams of fat a day. The first step, then, is to divide the 2.5 grams of Total Fat in the soup by 65.

$$2.5 \div 65 = 0.038$$

Next, multiply this number by 100 in order to change it to a percentage:

$$0.038 \times 100 = 3.8$$

Finally, round up that result to the nearest whole number:

$$4\%$$

So one serving of soup would contain about 4% of your total daily allowance of Fat. You can see that the math is correct, because the Nutrition Facts label lists the Daily Value for the Total Fat as 4%—the same number you came up with!

Sugars and Protein

You may have noticed that there are no numbers listed for sugars and protein. Sugars have no percentage listing because no reference value has ever been established for what a "good" or healthy amount of sugar in a day should be. Meanwhile, unless a food is claimed to be high in protein (or if it is made for infants, like jars of baby food), manufacturers are not actually required to list a number for protein.

Scientists have never determined what a healthy amount of sugar is. Although it provides quick energy, sugar is probably healthiest in small amounts.

CONCLUSION

The next time you step into your kitchen, you will see it in a brand new way. This is because you now know how much math is going on in that room! From refrigeration to cooking, food has a lot more to do with math than you probably ever realized.

How about the supermarket? The next time you go there with your mother or father, look at all the different food labels. Maybe you can even teach your parents how to read them!

And now that you really understand measuring, maybe you'll try to do some cooking. Since you now know how to alter food recipes, you can cook for as many or as few people as necessary!

All this talk about food has probably made you hungry. Now that you have read this book, are your food choices going to be any different than they were?

What are you going to eat today? ▶

GLOSSARY

Bacteria – Very small organisms that can grow in food and cause people to become sick

Calories – The amount of heat needed to raise the temperature of 1 gram of pure water 1 degree centigrade

Digested – When the stomach breaks down food to be used by the body as fuel

Dividend – The number in a division problem that the divisor must be fitted into

Division – The opposite of multiplication; a method used to discover how many times one quantity is contained within another

Divisor – The number in a division problem that must be fitted into the dividend

Equation – A mathematical problem

Expiration date – The date at which a food spoils

Ingredients – The "building blocks" of a recipe

Measuring – Determining an exact amount of something

Metric System – The standard of measurement used by most of the world

Multiplicand – The number in a multiplication problem that is to be added to itself

Multiplication – A method for adding large groups of numbers

Multiplier – The number in a multiplication problem that specifies how many times the multiplicand is to be added to itself

Nutrients – Elements contained in food that enable the body to carry out its essential functions

Product – The result of a multiplication problem

Quotient – The result of a division problem

Recipe – A group of instructions that explain how to make something

Units of measure – Set quantities for either dry or liquid goods such as cup, tablespoon, pound, and ounce

Weight – A measure of how heavy something is

Further Reading

MacKey, Laura. *Math in the Kitchen (Math Is Everywhere Series)*. Evan-Moor Corp, 1994.

VanCleave, Janice. *Math for Every Kid*. John Wiley and Sons, 1991.

Zeman, Anne and Kate Kelly. *Everything You Need To Know About Math Homework*. Scholastic, 1994.

Websites to Visit

http://www.howstuffworks.com/food.htm

How Stuff Works – Food

http://www.wcsscience.com/room/temperature.html

Worsley School Online – What is "Room Temperature?"

http://vm.cfsan.fda.gov/label.html

U.S. Food and Drug Administration –

Food Labeling and Nutrition

http://www.howstuffworks.com/question670.htm

How Stuff Works - What are calories?

How are they measured in food?

http://www.infoplease.com/ipa/A0001661.html

InfoPlease – Metric and U.S. Equivalents

INDEX

bacteria   25, 28, 30

calories   34, 35, 36, 37, 38, 41

centigrade   36

conduction   28, 29

convection   28, 29

cooking thermometer   29

diet   38, 41

dry quantities   15, 17, 20, 21

energy   5

expiration date   27

food labels   15

freezer   24, 25, 26, 27

grams   20, 22, 35, 42

heat transfer   28

ingredients   7, 8, 9, 10, 11, 12, 13, 14, 34

liquid quantities   15, 16, 20

liters   20, 22

measuring   8, 15, 44

metric system   20, 21, 22, 23, 36

microwave   31

nutrients   34, 40, 41

Nutrition Facts labels   34, 35, 36, 40, 42

nutritional labels   33

nutritional value   33

oven   30

radiation (heat)   28, 31

radio waves   31

recipe   7, 8, 9, 10, 11, 13, 44

refrigerator   24, 25, 26, 27

room temperature   25, 26

serving size   34, 35

stove   29, 31

temperature   28, 30, 36

U.S. Customary System   20, 21

units of measure   10

weight   18, 19

weight label   17

About The Author

Kieran Walsh has written a variety of children's nonfiction books, primarily on historical and social studies topics, including the recent Rourke series *Holiday Celebrations* and *Countries In the News*. He divides his time between upstate New York and New York City.